MW00441897

For the Teacher

This reproducible study guide to use in conjunction with the novel *The Tiger Rising* consists of lessons for guided reading. Written in chapter-by-chapter format, the guide contains a synopsis, pre-reading activities, vocabulary and comprehension exercises, as well as extension activities to be used as follow-up to the novel.

In a homogeneous classroom, whole class instruction with one title is appropriate. In a heterogeneous classroom, reading groups should be formed: each group works on a different novel at its own reading level. Depending upon the length of time devoted to reading in the classroom, each novel, with its guide and accompanying lessons, may be completed in three to six weeks.

Begin using NOVEL-TIES for reading development by distributing the novel and a folder to each child. Distribute duplicated pages of the study guide for students to place in their folders. After examining the cover and glancing through the book, students can participate in several pre-reading activities. Vocabulary questions should be considered prior to reading a chapter; all other work should be done after the chapter has been read. Comprehension questions can be answered orally or in writing. The classroom teacher should determine the amount of work to be assigned, always keeping in mind that readers must be nurtured and that the ultimate goal is encouraging students' love of reading.

The benefits of using NOVEL-TIES are numerous. Students read good literature in the original, rather than in abridged or edited form. The good reading habits, formed by practice in focusing on interpretive comprehension and literary techniques, will be transferred to the books students read independently. Passive readers become active, avid readers.

Novel-Ties® are printed on recycled paper.

The purchase of this study guide entitles an individual teacher to reproduce pages for use in a classroom. Reproduction for use in an entire school or school system or for commercial use is prohibited. Beyond the classroom use by an individual teacher, reproduction, transmittal or retrieval of this work is prohibited without written permission from the publisher.

Copyright © 2007 by LEARNING LINKS INC.

SYNOPSIS

Rob Horton is a lonely boy who has recently moved with his father to Lister, a small Florida town, following the death of Rob's mother. They live at the Kentucky Star Hotel, where Mr. Horton is employed as the maintenance man. Mr. Horton, deeply unhappy at the turn his life has taken, seems to be trying to erase the memory of his late wife. But Rob cannot forget: he whispers the name of his mother when nobody is around to hear it and recalls the golden days of his childhood.

Life in Lister is gloomy and difficult. A pair of brothers bully and attack Rob every day on the school bus. Rob's legs have broken out in a rash that won't go away. But then, two wonderful things happen: he discovers a caged tiger in the woods, and a defiant girl named Sistine Bailey moves to Lister and joins Rob's sixth-grade class. Like Rob, Sistine is an outsider and a target for the bullies. But unlike Rob, she is full of fight and never runs away when provoked. She hates the town of Lister and is waiting desperately for her father to come and take her away to a new life. Willie May, a wise woman who works as a maid at the Kentucky Star, declares that Rob and Sistine are a pair: one full of sorrow, the other full of rage.

Mr. Beauchamp, the motel owner, tells Rob that he owns the tiger and requires Rob to feed the tiger each day. Afraid to refuse because it could put his father's job in jeopardy, Rob gains possession of the keys to the tiger's cage. He is fascinated by the proud beast that seems to suffer in the same way that Rob suffers, with all of its power trapped inside, just waiting to explode. What if someone should open the door of that cage and let the tiger out? What if Rob let his own feelings out?

After an uneasy beginning, Rob and Sistine become friends. He has never met anyone quite like this yellow-haired girl, with her knowledge of Italian art, her love of beauty, and her passion for freedom and justice. He finds himself telling her things that nobody else in Lister knows about him: how his mother died, why he loves to carve objects out of wood, and finally, where the tiger's cage is located. Immediately, Sistine becomes determined to free the tiger.

For the sake of Sistine's friendship and a desire to do a noble act, Rob opens the tiger's cage and releases the animal. Willie May, who feared that Rob might give the tiger its freedom without considering the danger, brings Rob's father into the woods. Upon seeing the wild animal running loose, he shoots the tiger. Moved to fury, Rob accuses his father of stifling him, and of trying to erase the past. When the emotional storm passes, father and son have gained a deeper understanding of each other. No matter what the future brings, they will be able to face it together.

PRE-READING QUESTIONS AND ACTIVITIES

1. Preview the book by reading the title and the author's name and by looking at the illustration on the cover. What do you think the book is about? Do you think it takes place in the city or the country? Have you read any other books by the same author?

2. In this novel, a character keeps powerful feelings locked up inside him. Make a list of the times when you kept an emotion to yourself. In each case, how did you feel?

3. If you were to dream up the perfect friend, what would this person be like? What special qualities would he or she possess? Would this person be very much like you or very different? Make a list of the characteristics that you think the ideal friend should have.

4. Have you read any other books or stories that deal with the lives of children who have lost a parent to death or divorce? Jot down whatever you can remember from your reading. When you finish reading *The Tiger Rising*, compare the facts and observations in your notes to those you discovered while reading the book.

5. **Science Connection:** In this novel, a tiger is kept in a cage. Do some research to find out about the needs of wild animals kept in captivity. What special problems arise when a wild creature is caged? Based on your reading, do you think people should keep these animals in captivity?

6. **Cooperative Learning Activity:** Work with a small group of classmates to discuss the problem of bullying at school and in the community and its possible solutions. As you read this book, notice how bullying affects the two main characters.

7. With a partner, discuss problems that can arise when someone moves to a new community and attends a new school. How would you expect a person who enters such an unfamiliar environment to feel? Have you ever had such an experience?

8. **Art Connection:** Do some research to learn about the Sistine Chapel and Michelangelo, the artist who created the famous artwork on the chapel's ceiling. Find some illustrations and share them with your classmates.

9. Read the statements in the Anticipation Guide on page three of this study guide. In the "You" column, place a check [✔] next to each statement with which you agree. When you finish the story, place a check next to each statement with which you think the author would agree.

10. As you read *The Tiger Rising*, fill in the story map on page four of this study guide.

Pre-Reading Questions and Activities (cont.)

ANTICIPATION GUIDE

Statement	You	Author
1. If you ignore a bully, he or she will go away.		
2. The best way to react to a bully is to fight.		
3. Crying is a good way to release feelings of sadness.		
4. It is important to hide feelings of grief from others.		
5. People who are the targets of bullying deserve the treatment they receive.		
6. Wild animals should not be put in cages.		
7. It is unkind to release a caged animal into the wild.		
8. It is possible for a former enemy to become a good friend.		
9. Parents and teachers are responsible for the physical and emotional health of the children in their care.		
10. A person with a contagious disease should be isolated from the community.		

Pre-Reading Questions and Activities (cont.)

STORY MAP

Title _____

Author _____

Main Characters	Descriptions

Plot—Main Events

First, _____

Then, _____

Next, _____

Finally, _____

Theme—Message

This story taught me that _____

_____

_____

CHAPTERS 1 – 6

Vocabulary: Draw a line from each word on the left to its definition on the right. Then use the numbered words to fill in the blanks in the sentences below.

1. abiding
2. astounded
3. eager
4. sullen
5. ignorant
6. defiantly
7. buoyed

a. gloomy or sulky
b. kept afloat
c. lacking knowledge or education
d. enthusiastic or impatient
e. continuing; permanent
f. very surprised
g. with boldness or an attitude of resistance

. . . .

1. When I told my sister that the party was canceled, she gave me a(n) _____ glance and went up to her room.

2. "I won't obey a foolish order, Captain!" the sailor declared _____.

3. The math quiz did not go very well, but I was _____ by the teacher's promise to let us take the quiz again.

4. The farmer cannot afford to be _____ of weather conditions.

5. Because of her _____ fear of snakes, my mother never set foot in the woods behind our house.

6. On Susan's first camping trip, she was _____ to see a small brown bear poking its head through the flap of the tent.

7. We were _____ to see the new playground and try out the equipment.

Read to find out why Rob dreads school.

Questions:

1. Why did Rob and his father move to Lister?

2. How did Rob discover a live tiger?

Chapters 1 – 6 (cont.)

3. Why did Rob want to avoid the school bus?

4. In what way was Sistine Bailey a surprise to the sixth graders in Mrs. Soames's class?

5. Why did Rob feel free once he left the principal's office?

6. How did Rob save Sistine from the bullies in the cafeteria?

Questions for Discussion:

1. Do you agree with Rob's father that it does no good to cry over a loss?

2. Why do you think the author chose to begin the story *after* Rob discovered the tiger?

3. In your opinion, what is the best way to deal with bullies? Would you have acted like Rob or Sistine if you were faced with bullies?

4. Why do you imagine Rob had developed a way of not thinking about certain things? Do you suppose this helped him, or hurt him?

Literary Devices:

I. *Hook*—A hook in literature refers to a passage at the beginning of a book that demands the reader's attention and encourages the reader to continue on in the book. What is the hook at the beginning of this book?

_____

_____

II. *Personification*—Personification is a device in which an author grants human qualities to things that are not human. For example:

   Fog was hugging the ground.

   What is being personified?

_____

_____

   How does the use of personification help you visualize the scene?

_____

_____

Chapters 1 – 6 (cont.)

III. *Simile*—A simile is a figure of speech in which two objects are compared using the words "like" or "as." For example:

> He specifically did not think about Norton and Billy Threemonger waiting for him like chained and starved guard dogs, eager to attack.

What is being compared?

_____

Why is this an apt comparison?

_____

_____

IV. *Metaphor*—A metaphor is an implied comparison between unlike objects. An extended metaphor refers to a comparison that continues on in the book. For example:

> Rob had a way of not thinking about things. He imagined himself as a suitcase that was too full, like the one that he had packed when they left Jacksonville after the funeral. He made all his feelings go inside the suitcase; he stuffed them in tight and then sat on the suitcase and locked it shut . . . . Sometimes it was hard to keep the suitcase shut.

What is being compared?

_____

Why is this an apt comparison?

_____

_____

Writing Activities:

1. Write about a time when someone treated you unfairly. What happened? How did you react?

2. Suppose you found a caged tiger in your town. What would you do? Write a story about you and the tiger, including descriptive details. Be sure your story has a clear beginning, middle, and end.

CHAPTERS 7 – 10

Vocabulary: Synonyms are words with similar meanings. Draw a line from each word in column A to its synonym in column B. Then use the words in column A to fill in the blanks in the sentences below.

	A			B
1.	extraordinary		a.	curl
2.	permanent		b.	image
3.	vision		c.	unusual
4.	slathered		d.	wild
5.	desperate		e.	constant
6.	adjusted		f.	spread
7.	swirl		g.	fixed

. . . .

1. After his fight with the neighborhood dog, my bold cat walked with a
    _____ limp.

2. Joey _____ his toast with peanut butter and took a huge bite.

3. I _____ my umbrella so that it would keep the slanting rain out of my
    eyes.

4. Just before Sarah blew out her candles, she had a(n) _____ of the
    bicycle she wanted for her birthday.

5. "It is most _____ for snow to fall in April," my grandmother commented.

6. With a(n) _____ cry, the man jumped from the sinking ship into the
    waiting lifeboat.

7. Seated around the crackling campfire, we watched the smoke _____ up
    into the dark sky.

> Read to find out how Rob spends his days away from school.

Chapters 7 – 10 (cont.)

Questions:

1. What advice did Sistine offer Rob about the children on the bus and their classmates?

2. Why did Rob tell Sistine all he knew about the Sistine Chapel?

3. Why did Sistine touch the rash on Rob's legs?

4. Why was Rob relieved when the Threemonger brothers came to beat him up on the bus?

5. Why did it take so long for Rob's father to comment on the note from the principal ?

6. Why did Mr. Horton allow Rob to stay home for a few days?

7. Why did Rob assume Mr. Beauchamp was very rich?

8. According to Rob, why couldn't he determine in advance the object he was about to whittle?

9. Why did Willie May tell Rob "to let the sadness rise"?

Questions for Discussion:

1. Why do you think Rob was able to discuss his life with Sistine?

2. Why do you think Rob associated Sistine and the tiger in his dreams?

3. Do you think Sistine was right when she advised Rob not to run away from bullies?

4. How do you imagine living in a motel affected Rob's self image?

5. Whom do you think Rob might tell about the Tiger?

Literary Devices:

I. *Symbol*—A symbol is an object, person, or event that represents an idea or set of ideas. What did the tiger symbolize?

_____

_____

What did the tiger symbolize in Rob's dream?

_____

_____

Chapters 7 – 10 (cont.)

II. *Simile*—What is being compared in the following simile?

> He opened his mouth and the words fell out, one on top of the other, like gold coins.

_____

Why is this simile better than saying "Rob could not stop talking"?

_____

_____

_____

III. *Point of View*—Point of view refers to the person who is telling a story. We learn about people and events through this person's eyes. The story may be narrated by a character in the story (first-person narrative) or by the author (third-person narrative). From whose point of view is this story told?

_____

Why do you think the author chose this point of view?

_____

_____

Literary Elements:

I. *Vernacular*—A writer may use vernacular, the nonstandard language of a place or group, to show how people actually speak. For example:

> "That stuff ain't nothing anybody else can catch," his father said.

What does this passage reveal about Rob's father?

_____

_____

What other example of vernacular can you find in this part of the story? Who is speaking?

_____

_____

Chapters 7 – 10 (cont.)

II. *Characterization*—In the Venn diagram below, compare the characters of Rob and Sistine. Record the events and the personality traits they have in common in the overlapping part of the circles. Add information as you continue to read the book.

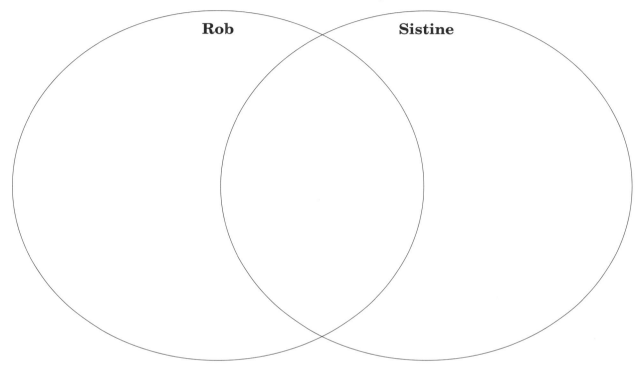

Rob   **Sistine**

Writing Activities:

1. Write about a time when you made a friend when you least expected to. Describe the circumstances in which this friendship began. What drew you and this person together?

2. Imagine that you are Sistine Bailey. Write a diary entry telling how you felt as you sat with Rob Horton on the bus and talked about important things.

CHAPTERS 11 – 14

Vocabulary: Use the words from the Word Box and the clues below to complete the crossword puzzle.

WORD BOX					
culture	demanded	enormous	sculptor	trespassing	wary
delicate	determined	relief	stance	us	

Across
1. dainty; fragile
5. entering a private area unlawfully
6. person who creates sculptures
9. objective pronoun referring to two or more people
10. asked for urgently; claimed
11. cautious; alert

Down
2. huge
3. viewpoint
4. showing a fixed purpose
7. knowledge of intellectual or artistic accomplishments
8. freedom from pain or discomfort

Read to find out if there is really a tiger in the woods.

Chapters 11 – 14 (cont.)

Questions:

1. How was it revealed that Sistine had another run-in with the bullies at school?

2. How did the Kentucky Star Motel get its name?

3. Why did Rob decide to tell Sistine about the tiger?

4. What did Sistine realize about Rob when she saw his tray of wooden carvings? How did this help her to understand him better?

5. Why did Rob become sad when Sistine talked about her parents' separation?

6. Why did Sistine become annoyed with Rob? What made her forgive him?

7. What was Sistine's reaction to the caged tiger? What did this reveal about her?

Questions for Discussion:

1. What do you think that Sistine concluded after she saw the place where Rob lived?

2. Do you think that Sistine and Rob should free the tiger?

3. Why do you think Rob experienced happiness when he and Sistine visited the tiger?

Literary Devices:

I. *Personification*—What is being personified in the following passage?

> Rob felt a familiar loneliness rise up and drape its arm over his shoulder.

_____

Why is this better than saying, "Rob was lonely"?

_____

II. *Simile*—What is being compared in the following passage?

> She let him hold on to her hand. It was an impossibly small and bony hand, as delicate as the skeleton of a baby bird.

_____

Why is this better than saying, "She let him hold her small, bony hand"?

_____

Chapters 11 – 14 (cont.)

Poetry Connection:

Read the following complete poem by William Blake, "The Tiger." Write a response to the poem. Share your writing with a group of classmates.

THE TIGER

Tiger, tiger, burning bright
In the forests of the night,
What immortal hand or eye
Could frame thy fearful symmetry?

In what distant deeps or skies
Burnt the fire of thine eyes?
On what wings dare he aspire?
What the hand dare seize the fire?

And what shoulder and what art
Could twist the sinews of thy heart?
And when thy heart began to beat,
What dread hand and what dread feet?

What the hammer? what the chain?
In what furnace was thy brain?
What the anvil? What dread grasp
Dare its deadly terrors clasp?

When the stars threw down their spears,
And water'd heaven with their tears,
Did He smile His work to see?
Did He who made the lamb make thee?

Tiger, tiger, burning bright
In the forests of the night,
What immortal hand or eye
Dare frame thy fearful symmetry?

Writing Activity:

Using the poem "The Tiger" as a model, write about an animal that fascinates you. You may write in prose if you prefer.

CHAPTERS 15 – 20

Vocabulary: Read each group of words. Cross out the one that does not belong with the others. On the line below the words, tell how the remaining words are alike.

1. constellation   group   arrangement   object

    The other words are alike because _____

2. refused   allowed   forbidden   prevented

    The other words are alike because _____

3. complete   whole   entire   part

    The other words are alike because _____

4. fervently   warmly   feverishly   mildly

    The other words are alike because _____

5. shifted   dashed   skidded   swerved

    The other words are alike because _____

6. insist   require   demand   ask

    The other words are alike because _____

7. upset   discouraged   bold   dismayed

    The other words are alike because _____

8. squint   sniff   blink   wink

    The other words are alike because _____

> Read to find out how Rob gets the keys to the tiger's cage.

Questions:

1. Why did Rob's feelings of happiness disappear as soon as he returned to the motel with Sistine?
2. Why did the world seem dark to Rob ever since his mother died?
3. Why was Sistine's mother distressed when she came to pick up Sistine at the motel?
4. Why did Rob whisper his mother's name over and over again?

Chapters 15 – 20 (cont.)

5. What did Willie May mean when she said, "Who don't know something in a cage?"
6. Why did Beauchamp drive Rob into the woods?
7. Why was Rob frightened by the responsibility of carrying the keys to the tiger cage?
8. Why did Sistine cry when Rob refused to open the tiger cage?

Questions for Discussion:

1. Consider the episode in which Sistine asked for money for the telephone. Do you think she was being rude or spunky? In your opinion, should she have acted this way?
2. Why do you suppose Rob's father was suspicious of Rob's good mood? What experiences might have caused him to feel this way?
3. Why do you think Sistine was angry with her mother?
4. Why do you think Willie May told Rob the story about the parakeet?
5. Do you agree with Rob's father that they should not talk about Caroline in order to get on with their lives?
6. If you were in Rob's place, would you open the cage and set the tiger free?

Literary Devices:

I. *Metaphor*—A metaphor is a suggested or implied comparison between two unlike objects. For example:

> There was a single crack and the bird was suspended in midair, pinned for a moment to the sky with his father's bullet.

What is being compared?

_____

_____

II. *Onomatopoeia*—Onomatopoeia is a literary device in which a word imitates a sound found in nature. For instance, the word *crash* imitates the sound of one object hitting another. Which word in the sentence below is an example of onomatopoeia?

> It hurt the back of Rob's throat to think about that now, to think about the gun and his mother and the small thud the bird made when it hit the ground.

_____

Why is it better than saying, " the bird hit the ground with a dull sound"?

_____

_____

Chapters 15 – 20 (cont.)

Literary Element: Setting

Setting refers to the time and place where the events of a novel occur. What is the setting of *The Tiger Rising*?

_____

How does the setting shape the events in the novel?

_____

_____

Art Connection:

Create an artwork that shows the tiger in his cage. You might make a drawing, painting, collage, or sculpture of the tiger. Place your artwork in the classroom so that others can enjoy it.

Science Connection:

Do some research to find out why tigers are an endangered species. What factors threaten their existence? How can people help? Prepare an oral report and share your ideas with a group of classmates.

Writing Activity:

Write a journal entry about a time when you or someone you know was given a big responsibility. How did you manage to handle this responsibility? What did you learn from the experience?

CHAPTER 21 – 25

Vocabulary: Use a word from the Word Box to replace the underlined word or phrase in each of the sentences below. Write the word on the line below the sentence.

WORD BOX		
dusk	original	reproachful
materialized	recalled	seep

1. We heard the soft sound of hooves, and then the deer <u>appeared</u> in the clearing by the stream.

   _____

2. There are many versions of this fairy tale, but the <u>first</u> story was told long ago in China.

   _____

3. Before Dad fixed the pipe, water used to <u>spread slowly</u> from it onto the bathroom floor.

   _____

4. When it is <u>just before nightfall</u>, you can see many fireflies in our yard.

   _____

5. The teacher gave the student a <u>full of blame</u> look as she handed back the incomplete homework paper.

   _____

6. Just before I fell asleep, I <u>remembered</u> a pleasant day at the beach.

   _____

> Read to find out whether Rob and Sistine free the tiger.

Questions:

1. Why did Willie May think that Sistine needed to deal with her anger?
2. Why did Willie May say that Rob and Sistine were "some pair"?
3. What advice did Willie May give Sistine? What did she want Sistine to understand?
4. Why didn't Rob admit to his father that the meat was for the tiger?
5. Why did the carving of Cricket make Willie May feel better?
6. Why did Willie May discourage Sistine from freeing the tiger?

Chapter 21 – 25 (cont.)

Questions for Discussion:

1. Why do you think Sistine was in so many fights?

2. Do you think Rob's father was different when his wife was alive?

3. What do you suppose made Rob sense that Sistine's father was never coming to get her?

4. What do you think Rob planned to do next?

Literary Devices:

I. *Hyperbole*—Hyperbole is a figure of speech in which there is an intentional exaggeration. For example:

> You angry. You got all the anger in the world inside you.
> I know angry when I meet it.

Why do you think Willie May used hyperbole when she spoke to Sistine?

_____

_____

II. *Simile*—What is being compared in the following simile?

> She turned and walked away, and Rob stood and considered
> her words. He felt them on his skin like shards of broken glass.

_____

Why is this better than saying, "Rob was hurt by Sistine's words"?

_____

_____

III. *Cliffhanger*—A cliffhanger is a device borrowed from serialized silent films in which an episode ended at a moment of great suspense or tension. In a book, it usually appears at the end of a chapter to encourage the reader to continue on in the book. What is the cliffhanger at the end of Chapter Twenty-five?

_____

IV. *Symbolism*—What did Rob's carved cricket symbolize?

_____

_____

Writing Activity:

Write about a time when a friend or family member made you feel angry. Describe the situation and tell whether you expressed your feelings or kept them inside. How did anger shape your words and actions?

CHAPTERS 26 – 30

Vocabulary: Antonyms are words with opposite meanings. Draw a line from each word in column A to its antonym in column B. Then use the words in column A to fill in the blanks in the sentences below.

	A			B	
1.	emancipators		a.	regarded
2.	gratitude		b.	aware
3.	coward		c.	jailers
4.	furious		d.	hero
5.	ignored		e.	deny
6.	explosive		f.	pleased
7.	oblivious		g.	indifference
8.	admit		h.	calm

. . . .

1. The young girl burst into song on the bus, _____ of all the people who stared at her in amazement.

2. The audience became _____ when the concert was canceled.

3. The bumblebees _____ the paper flowers because they had no scent.

4. The volcano erupted with _____ force, spewing out tons of lava.

5. Once the video of the track meet was shown, everyone had to _____ that I won.

6. The captured soldiers thanked their _____, who freed them from prison and brought them home.

7. The young man refused to serve in the army even though he risked being called a(n) _____.

8. The new mayor expressed his _____ to the people who had voted for him.

> Read to find out whether the tiger is freed.

Chapters 26 – 30 (cont.)

Questions:

1. Why did Rob promise Sistine he was going to free the tiger?

2. Why was Sistine polite to Beauchamp? Why was Rob surprised by this behavior?

3. How did the tiger respond when Rob first opened the door? Why?

4. Why did Rob's father shoot the tiger?

5. Why did Rob's father quietly accept Rob's anger after the shooting?

6. What did Rob realize about his father after his anger left him?

7. How did Sistine feel about her own role in the events that caused the death of the tiger?

8. What did father and son realize about their relationship?

Questions for Discussion:

1. Would you have acted as Rob did when he freed the tiger?

2. What do you think Sistine learned from the death of the tiger?

3. Do you think Willie May should have brought Rob's father to the woods?

4. Why do you think it is important to express powerful feelings?

5. Why do you think it took the death of a tiger to bring about an expression of love between Rob and his father?

6. Why do you suppose the story ends before Beauchamp found out about the tiger's death?

Literary Devices:

I. *Metaphor*—What is being compared in the following metaphor:

> He opened the suitcase. And the words sprang out of it, coiled and explosive.

_____

What does this reveal about Rob's hidden feelings?

_____

_____

Chapters 26 – 30 (cont.)

II. *Symbol*—At the end of the story, what did the tiger symbolize?

_____

_____

What did the carved wooden bird symbolize?

_____

_____

Writing Activities:

1. Imagine that you are a news reporter. Write an article about the thrilling events that took place in the town of Lister when a wild tiger was released from its cage. Make your article detailed and precise so that the reader has a complete picture of what happened.

2. Write about a time when you suddenly understood how another person was feeling. What gave you this flash of understanding? How did it change your view of the other person?

CLOZE ACTIVITY

The following passage has been taken from Chapter One of the novel. Read it through completely, and then fill in each blank with a word that makes sense. Afterwards, you may compare your language with that of the author.

It was early morning and it looked like it might rain; it had been raining every day for almost two weeks. The sky was gray and the _____ [1] was thick and still. Fog was _____ [2] the ground. To Rob, it seemed _____ [3] if the tiger was some magic _____, [4] rising out of the mist. He _____ [5] so astounded at his discovery, so _____, [6] that he stood and stared. But _____ [7] for a minute; he was afraid _____ [8] look at the tiger for too _____, [9] afraid that the tiger would disappear. _____ [10] stared, and then he turned and _____ [11] back into the woods, toward the Kentucky _____. [12] And the whole way home, while _____ [13] brain doubted what he had seen, _____ [14] heart beat out the truth to _____. [15] *Ti-ger, Ti-ger, Ti-ger.*

That was what _____ [16] thought about as he stood beneath _____ [17] Kentucky Star sign and waited for the _____. [18] The tiger. He did not think _____ [19] the rash on his legs, the _____ [20] red blisters that snaked their way _____ [21] his shoes. His father said that it _____ [22] be less likely to itch if _____ [23] didn't think about it.

And he _____ [24] not think about his mother. He _____ [25] thought about her since the morning _____ [26] the funeral, the morning he couldn't _____ [27] crying the great heaving sobs that _____ [28] his chest and stomach hurt. His father, watching him, standing beside him, had started to cry, too.

POST-READING ACTIVITIES

1. Return to the Anticipation Guide that you began in the Pre-Reading Activities on page three of this study guide. Place a check next to each statement with which you think the author would agree.

2. Return to the story map that you began on page four of this study guide. Fill in additional information and compare your responses with those of your classmates.

3. Return to the Venn diagram that you began on page eleven of this study guide. Add more information about Rob and Sistine. Then compare your responses to those of your classmates.

4. In a story, a conflict is a struggle between two opposing forces. In *The Tiger Rising*, both Rob and Sistine have conflicts they try to resolve. Many stories present more than one conflict. Use a chart, such as the one below, to list the conflicts in *The Tiger Rising*. In the third column indicate whether each conflict was resolved and if so, how it was resolved.

Type of Conflict	Example	Resolution
person *vs.* person/society		
person *vs.* nature		
person *vs.* self (inner struggle)		

5. Reread the end of the last chapter in order to determine the significance of the Kentucky Star Motel and its neon sign.

6. Do you think *The Tiger Rising* would make a good film? If so, who should play the leading roles? What scenes would need to be changed or omitted? Are there any scenes that should be added? Create a poster for a film version of this book.

7. **Fluency/Readers Theater:** Read a chapter of the book that has a lot of dialogue among several characters. Each character's dialogue should be read by one student. The characters should read only those words inside the quotation marks. Ignore phrases such as "he said" or "she said." One student can read the narration. Use simple props, such as hats, to identify the characters.

Post-Reading Activities (cont.)

8. **Cooperative Learning Activity:** Work with a group of your classmates to find one or more passages in the book that convey a strong message or are meaningful in some way. Present these passages to the other groups in your class and tell why they have been selected. Compare your selections with those chosen by other groups. Were there any passages that were chosen by more than one group?

9. **Literature Circle:** Have a literature circle discussion in which you tell your personal reactions to *The Tiger Rising*. Here are some questions and sentence starters to help your literature circle begin a discussion.
   - Which character in the novel are you most like? The least?
   - Which character did you like the most? The least?
   - Did you find the characters in the novel realistic? Why or why not?
   - Who else would you like to read this novel? Why?
   - What questions would you like to ask the author about the novel?
   - It was not fair when . . .
   - I would have liked to see . . .
   - I wonder . . .
   - Rob learned that . . .
   - Sistine learned that . . .

SUGGESTIONS FOR FURTHER READING

Fiction

* Armstrong, William. *Sounder*. HarperCollins.
* Banks, Lynn Reid. The Indian in the Cupboard. HarperCollins.
* Burnett, Frances Hodgson. *The Secret Garden*. HarperCollins.

Byars, Betsy. *The Not-Just-Anybody Family*. Random House.

* Cleary, Beverly. *Dear Mr. Henshaw*. HarperCollins.
* Estes, Eleanor. *The Hundred Dresses*. Harcourt.
* George, Jean Craighead. *My Side of the Mountain*. Penguin.
* Holt, Kimberly Willis. *When Zachary Beaver Came to Town*. Random House.
* Naylor, Phyllis Reynolds. *Saving Shiloh*. Simon & Schuster.
* _____. *Shiloh*. Simon & Schuster.
* Rawlings, Majorie Kinnan. *The Yearling*. Simon & Schuster.
* Rawls, Wilson. *Where the Red Fern Grows*. Random House.

Rylant, Cynthia. *Every Living Thing*. Simon & Schuster.

* _____. *Missing May*. Random House.
* Paterson, Katherine. *Bridge to Terabithia*. HarperCollins.
* _____. *The Great Gilly Hopkins*. HarperCollins.
* Patron, Susan. *The Higher Power of Lucky*. Simon & Schuster.
* Peck, Richard. *A Long Way from Chicago*. Penguin.

Sachs, Marilyn. *The Bear's House*. Dutton.

* Smith, Doris Buchanan. *A Taste of Blackberries*. HarperCollins.

Stolz, Mary. *A Dog on Barkham Street*. HarperCollins.

Townsend, John Rowe. *Dan Alone*. HarperCollins.

Nonfiction

LeShan, Eda. *Learning to Say Good-Bye: When a Parent Dies*. Simon & Schuster.

Some Other Books by Kate DiCamillo

* *Because of Winn-Dixie*. Candlewick Press.

Mercy Watson Goes For a Ride. Candlewick Press.

Mercy Watson to the Rescue. Candlewick Press.

The Miraculous Journey of Edward Tulane. Candlewick Press.

* *The Tale of Despereaux*. Candlewick Press.

* NOVEL-TIES study guides are available for these titles.

ANSWER KEY

Chapters 1 – 6

Vocabulary : 1. e 2. f 3. d 4. a 5. c 6. g 7. b; 1. sullen 2. defiantly 3. buoyed 4. ignorant 5. abiding 6. astounded 7. eager

Questions: 1. Rob and his father moved from Jacksonville to Lister after Rob's mother died: Rob's father thought they could put their sadness behind them and start a new life in a new place. 2. Rob discovered a live tiger in a cage when he was wandering in the woods. 3. Rob wanted to avoid the school bus because the aggressive Threemonger brothers would taunt and assault him. 4. Sistine Bailey was a surprise to the sixth graders in Mrs. Soames's class because she couldn't be taunted or bullied: instead, she acted as though she was contemptuous of Lister and its inhabitants. 5. Rob felt free because the principal sent him home until his skin rash cleared up, fearing it was contagious. Since Rob thought his rash would never clear, he was certain that he would never have to attend school again. 6. Rob saved Sistine from the bullies in the cafeteria by distracting them; he knew that they would follow him if he ran.

Chapters 7 – 10

Vocabulary: 1. c 2. e 3. b 4. f 5. d 6. g 7. a; 1. permanent 2. slathered 3. adjusted 4. vision 5. extraordinary 6. desperate 7. swirl

Questions: 1. Sistine advised Rob not to run away from the bullies because this would goad them on to further acts of aggression. 2. So that Sistine wouldn't think he was uncultured like the rest of the people in Lister, he told her everything he knew about the Sistine Chapel. 3. Sistine touched the rash on Rob's legs because she was hoping to catch an infectious disease that would keep her out of school and away from the bullies, too. 4. Rob was relieved when the Threemonger brothers came to beat him up on the bus because it interrupted an increasingly personal discussion with Sistine that he didn't know how to end. 5. It took a long time before Rob's father commented on the note because he was a poor reader and, therefore, struggled with the text. 6. Mr. Horton allowed Rob to stay home for a few days because he understood Rob was feeling overwhelmed by the bullies at school. 7. Rob thought that Mr. Beauchamp was very rich because he was most likely the owner of the caged tiger in back of the motel. 8. Rob never knew in advance what he was about to whittle because as his mother had always said, the piece of wood itself determines what the object will be. 9. Willie May told Rob "to let the sadness rise" because she understood that his physical symptom, the rash, was the outer manifestation of the grief he suppressed.

Chapters 11 – 14

Vocabulary: Across–1. delicate 5. trespassing 6. sculptor 9. us 10. demanded 11. wary; Down–2. enormous 3. stance 4. determined 7. culture 8. relief

Questions: 1. It was clear that Sistine had another run-in with the bullies when she arrived at Rob's motel wearing a dirty, torn dress and displaying bloody knuckles. 2. The Kentucky Star Motel was named after a racehorse Mr. Beauchamp had once owned. 3. Rob decided to tell Sistine about the tiger because he sensed that she would believe him and would want to see it, too. 4. When she saw this tray of wooden carvings, Sistine realized that Rob was an artist; this helped her to understand him better by showing her that Rob was sensitive and creative. 5. Rob became sad when Sistine talked about her parents' separation because she announced that she planned to leave Lister and live with her father. 6. Sistine became annoyed with Rob because he wouldn't share his private thoughts and feelings with her; she forgave him when he shared the deep hurt that his mother was dead. 7. When Sistine saw the tiger, she wanted to let it out of its cage; her reaction showed that she cherished freedom.

Chapters 15 – 20

Vocabulary: 1. object–the other words are alike because they all refer to a pattern of multiple objects 2. allowed–the other words are alike because they all mean "banned" 3. part–the other words are alike because they all refer to something complete 4. mildly–the other words are alike because they all mean "heatedly" 5. dashed–the other words are alike because they are all verbs meaning to turn or move away from 6. ask– the other words are alike because they are all verbs meaning "to command" 7. bold–the other words are alike because they all indicate the state of being worried or disheartened 8. sniff–the other words are alike because they all describe an action performed by the eyes

Questions: 1. Rob's feelings of happiness disappeared when he returned to the motel with Sistine because his father seemed suspicious and displeased at Rob for bringing home a girl, particularly since she was wearing his son's clothing. 2. Rob's world became dark after his mother died because she was a cheerful and optimistic person who lit up the world around her both literally and figura-

tively. Now, living with his sullen, pessimistic father, everything seemed dark. 3. Sistine's mother was distressed to find her daughter on the outskirts of town dressed in boy's clothes in the company of a boy she did not know. 4. Rob whispered his mother's name over and over again because he was trying to let out his feelings without upsetting his father. 5. When she said, "Who don't know something in a cage?" Willie May meant that people, too, were trapped by their circumstances. 6. Beauchamp drove Rob into the woods to show him the tiger and give him the job of feeding the tiger. 7. Rob was frightened by the responsibility of carrying the keys to the tiger cage because he knew that Sistine would try to talk him into opening the cage and letting the tiger go free. 8. Sistine cried when Rob refused to open the tiger cage because she identified with the tiger's predicament and could not control her feelings of frustration and resentment.

Chapters 21 – 25

Vocabulary: 1. materialized 2. original 3. seep 4. dusk 5. reproachful 6. recalled

Questions: 1. Willie May believed that Sistine needed to deal with her anger or it would eat away at her and that this would ruin her life. 2. Willie May said that Rob and Sistine were "some pair" because both were dominated by negative emotions that were harmful to them. 3. Willie May advised Sistine to rescue herself rather than wait for someone else to do it; she meant that Sistine would have to relinquish her hope for her father's return and deal with her own problems by herself. 4. Rob didn't tell his father the truth about the meat because his father seemed dangerous when he was in a rage. 5. The carving of Cricket made Willie May feel better because it restored her memory of the bird she had set free; having the little carving allowed her to retain the memory. 6. Willie May discouraged Sistine from freeing the tiger because practical concerns outweighed idealism: a freed tiger, unlike a freed parakeet, represented a grave danger.

Chapters 26 – 30

Vocabulary: 1. c 2. g 3. d 4. f 5. a 6. h 7. b 8. e; 1. oblivious 2. furious 3. ignored 4. explosive 5. admit 6. emancipators 7. coward 8. gratitude

Questions: 1. Rob promised Sistine he was going to free the tiger because he realized nothing meant more to him than her friendship and respect. 2. Sistine was polite to Beauchamp because she wanted him to think she was just an average girl, incapable of setting a tiger free; Rob was surprised by this behavior because normally Sistine spoke her mind to the point of rudeness. 3. The tiger didn't leave the cage when Rob first opened the door; it took some minutes for it to realize it was free. 4. Rob's father shot the tiger because he feared his son would be in danger. 5. After the shooting, Rob's father quietly accepted Rob's anger because he knew his son was overwhelmed by feelings of hurt and loss. 6. After his anger left him, Rob realized that his father was a complicated person who could both hurt and comfort, and that he too deeply missed Caroline. 7. When the tiger was shot, Sistine felt sorry and guilty for forcing Rob to set the events in motion that led to its death. 8. Father and son realized that their relationship was one of mutual need and dependency, and that they did not need to shut out the memory of the woman they had both loved.